CHESTER
City Beautiful

CHESTER
City Beautiful

Alistair and Jan Campbell

breedon **books**
PUBLISHING

First published in Great Britain in 2008 by
The Breedon Books Publishing Company Limited
Breedon House, 3 The Parker Centre,
Derby, DE21 4SZ.

A catalogue record for this book is available from
the British Library.

ISBN 978-1-85983-613-2

Printed and bound in Croatia.

CONTENTS

DEDICATION

This publication is dedicated to our family, friends and colleagues.

'Absent friends and those at sea.'

Eaton Hall
Chester
CH4 9ET

FOREWORD

By His Grace the Duke of Westminster KG OBE TD DL

Globally acknowledged as a truly alluring city, Chester richly deserves both its ancient and modern reputation as a highly desirable and popular visitor destination. Chester's history and heritage provides period architecture and unique streets, and of course the renowned Chester Rows.

It is difficult to ignore the city's appeal when its beauty is captured in photographic form. There are so many pleasing scenes and landmarks to entirely satisfy any professional or amateur photographer's desire to produce an image that is worthy of note. However, regardless of the city's charm, rarely has a publication contained so many images that bring the city to life and are worthy of comment and accolade.

Chester City Beautiful has been compiled by Cheshire-based husband and wife team Alistair and Jan Campbell, who collectively have over 50 years, professional photographic experience. Their professionalism and talent is clearly evident throughout this publication.

Chester City Beautiful will serve as both an inspirational aide memoire and provide nostalgic memories of what you have already seen or enthusiasm for what you are about to see.

The Duke of Westminster KG OBE TD DL

Glasgow

London

Cardiff

www.

UKCity
Images
.com

UK City Images is an elite and independent image library that specialises in providing the travel and media industries with high-quality photographs of UK city scenes and landmarks.

Portraying the richness and diversity of UK city architecture helps promote Britain as a desirable tourist destination, to both a global and British audience. Images are captured in a style that is deliberately designed to excite positive interest in its location and history.

All images within this publication are the sole copyright of UK City Images, who are pleased to offer a facility to purchase either print or data copies to both commercial and private customers. Sales enquiries should be directed to sales@ukcityimages.com.

An exciting array of other UK city scenes and landmarks, plus additional Chester images, can be viewed on our website at www.ukcityimages.com.

Liverpool

Birmingham

Newcastle

Portsmouth

8

INTRODUCTION

Antiqui Colant Antiquum Dierum
(Let the Ancients Worship the Ancient of Days)

Located within the county of Cheshire and in close proximity to the North Wales border, the City of Chester owes much of its status as a prominent and favoured tourist destination to its long and enthralling history.

Deva, one of three Roman legionary fortresses in Britain, was established in the late 70s AD. The strategic military position and importance of the site was to become the foundation of Chester's future heritage, providing an almost 2,000-year chronological diary of life as a Cestrian. The city's autobiography spans the Roman, Saxon, Norman, mediaeval, Tudor, Stuart, Georgian and Victorian eras to the present day.

A stroll around the largest unbroken stretch of city walls in Britain will help unfold some of the city's history as a former major seaport, military garrison and city under siege. The influence of the city's heritage is very much evident throughout its streets, lanes and architecture, with its principal thoroughfares still bearing a strong resemblance to their original historic design. Its famous and unique two-tiered Rows continue to maintain the city's ancient reputation as a thriving commerce-based community. Neither the canal nor River Dee is now associated with the responsibility of supporting former shipbuilding and manufacturing industries, but their picturesque banks and locks provide an idyllic setting for an array of sporting and leisure activities.

Each page of *Chester City Beautiful* colourfully and aesthetically portrays a scene, personality, landmark or tradition associated with this unique and historic city. Collectively the images offer a creative perspective and stunning portfolio, which certifies that Chester is truly a 'City Beautiful'.

RIVER DEE

The River Dee's 70-mile journey from source to sea begins in North Wales. It's relatively short but impressive passage through Chester is via the Meadows, under the Queen's Park Suspension Bridge, flowing parallel to the Groves, surging over the Weir, passing below the Dee Bridge, meandering around the Racecourse and sweeping far beneath the Grosvenor Bridge before finally returning back into North Wales. The dramatic influence that the river has contributed to the city's history and fortune is not instantly obvious. However, the route is at the very least scenic and at times absolutely stunning, as the following images illustrate.

The river provides an ideal opportunity for leisure activity and is a popular venue for both rowers and canoeists.

Cattle graze freely upon the unique city-centre 24 hectare public recreation area known as 'the Meadows'. Due to the nature of the land and habitat it has been designated as a Site of Biological Importance.

Cattle grazing on the Meadows and in the River Dee with the river tour boat in the foreground.

Sunset over the River Dee with the Meadows in the background.

Grosvenor Rowing Club.

The Riverside Promenade begins, or ends, at the Grosvenor Rowing Club with its pedestrianised route running parallel to the river for approximately two miles. The Groves section of the promenade is home to an abundance of small cafés and restaurants, which offer a selection of fine food and excellent views of the river and its many waterborne activities.

The Queen's Park Suspension Bridge was completed in 1923 and is the only footbridge over Chester's span of the Dee. The bridge has become a familiar landmark of the city and has been the backdrop for many television productions. Its metal structure is adorned with a variety of crests/coat of arms, including those of the City of Chester and Ranulf, the 2nd Earl of Chester (1128–1153).

The Groves and Queen's Park Suspension Bridge
viewed from the south bank of the river.

Crest of Ranulf, the 2nd Earl of Chester.

The Chester coat of arms.

Queen's Park Bridge with the *Lady Diana Showboat* passing underneath.

The Anchorite's Cell is also known as 'the Hermitage'. This dates back to the 14th century when it was a religious retreat for a reclusive monk or hermit. However, it may date back further due to a unsubstantiated local legend which states that King Harold did not die at the Battle of Hastings in 1066, but lived as a hermit in the Anchorite Cell.

Opposite: Leading past the Anchorite Cell from Grosvenor Park to the Groves.

Victorian bandstand at The Groves.

The banks of the Groves offer ample opportunity for nautical adventures with River Dee cruise trips, paddle, rowing and motorboat hire, pictured here and overleaf.

Constructed in around 1092, the Norman weir provided a head of water to power grinding wheels at the flour mills. The weir still performs a functional purpose, diverting water to the pumping station, and helps to maintain upstream water levels.

Part of the migration route for Atlantic salmon, the River Dee's Salmon Steps, also known as the Salmon Leap, were constructed in the early 20th century. The steps help the fish negotiate the weir and reach their spawning ground in the headwaters of the River Dee.

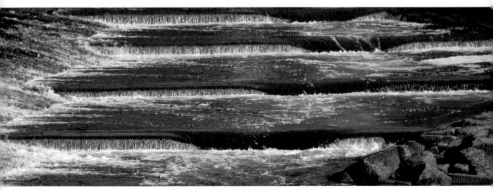

Built in around 1387 the Old Dee Bridge is a Grade I Listed Scheduled Ancient Monument and an important mediaeval city landmark. Extending from Bridgegate to Handbridge, the bridge still retains its tollgate post, where tolls were charged for crossing until 1885.

Opposite: Constructed in 1913, the hydro-electric Power Station at Castle Drive is believed to be the first of its type to supply electric power to an English city by utilising both tidal and headwaters to generate electricity. Decommissioned as a hydro-electric plant in 1951, the facility is now used for water extraction.

The Roodee once hosted a major sea port with an impressive ship-building industry. A miniature antique silver paddle held at the Town Hall is a declaration that the Lord Mayor of Chester retains the ancient title of Admiral of the Dee.

Situated on the former Roman port, Chester Racecourse is reputed to be the oldest racecourse in England, with regular race meetings since 1540.

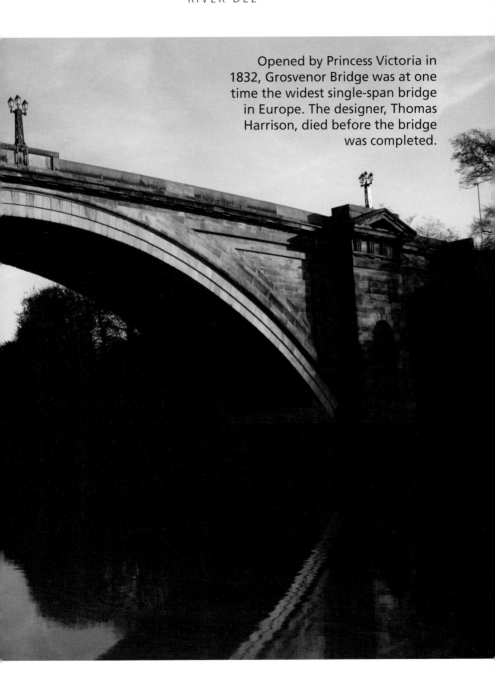

Opened by Princess Victoria in 1832, Grosvenor Bridge was at one time the widest single-span bridge in Europe. The designer, Thomas Harrison, died before the bridge was completed.

THE STREETS AND ROWS

Chester's street pattern still bears a striking resemblance to its original Roman and mediaeval layout. The High Cross is considered as the centre of the city where Eastgate, Northgate, Watergate and Bridge Street converge. Renowned for its black and white timber-framed building façades, each of these four arterial streets contributes to a Tudor appearance that is prevalent throughout the city. However, there is a definite architectural contrast, with each street having its own history, landmarks, character and tales to tell. The familiar topic along each route is undoubtedly retail and leisure. This traditionally commerce-based city centre is strongly supported by Chester's unique two-tier shopping levels known as the Rows. With the exception of Northgate Street the Rows can be found on both sides of each street.

EASTGATE STREET

Eastgate Street (opposite) is a mixture of contrasting architectural building styles, which are now home to many popular retail outlets, banks and building societies. The street has been compared with London's Regent Street and its largest department store, Browns of Chester (Debenhams), is known as the 'Harrods of the North'. The area is partially pedestrianised with restricted vehicle access, allowing the easy ebb and flow of workers and shoppers. There are normally a few talented buskers to keep visitors and locals entertained.

The Chester Grosvenor Hotel and Spa with the Eastgate Clock.

Lord Mayor's Parade on Eastgate Street. All along the street protrude a number of former tramway brackets that were used to power the electric trams until their replacement by buses in 1930. The brackets are now being used to suspend shop and hotel signs.

Opposite: Designed by John Douglas, the Eastgate Clock is arguably Chester's most famous landmark. Erected in 1899 to commemorate Queen Victoria's 1897 Diamond Jubilee, the aesthetic open wrought-iron structure makes it difficult to resist the temptation of a quick photograph, helping to confirm its reputation as the most photographed clock, after Big Ben, in the world.

The 5-Star Chester Grosvenor Hotel and Spa is owned by the Duke of Westminster. Non-residents are welcome to attend the hotel's traditional Afternoon Tea, which is gracefully served in its elegant Library Lounge.

Chester Grosvenor and Spa sign.

The Eastgate entrance to The Mall Grosvenor Shopping Centre.

An evening view of the Grosvenor Hotel and Spa with the Eastgate clock in the background.

Internal view of the Eastgate entrance to The Mall, Chester.

Opposite: The north side of Eastgate Street illustrating the contrasting building façades and architecture.

Below: The Eastgate Street and Row entrances to Browns of Chester.

Eastgate Rows and a former public house crown and glove sign that hangs above the Row.

Established in 1643, Ye Olde Boot Inn is one of the oldest surviving public houses in Chester.

Eastgate Street from
Bridge Street Row.

WATERGATE STREET

Watergate Street leads from the High Cross to the Watergate and Chester Racecourse via New Crane Street. Outlets along the street and Rows are very diverse, with goods and services ranging from vintners, silverware, antiques, art galleries, jewellers and furniture to excellent public houses, restaurants, cafés and bistros. Watergate Street has some magnificent period architecture which is of particular significance.

Watergate Street at the High Cross, viewed from the galleried Rows at the junction of Bridge Street and Eastgate Street.

God's Providence House, originally built in 1652, was rebuilt much later with the intention of retaining some semblance of its original façade. The house name and external inscription 'God's Providence is Mine Inheritance' are said to have originated from a family who survived the plague.

Watergate Street viewed from the south side of Watergate Row, with the High Cross and Eastgate Street in the background.

Leche House, a mediaeval town house, is the former Hand and Snatch public house that is now being utilised as a furniture showroom.

Evening view of the north side of Watergate Street Rows.

The timber-framed Bishop Lloyd's Palace was built for George Lloyd, Bishop of Sodor and Man (an historic diocese of the Church of England) and also Bishop of Chester, 1605–15. The building was originally completed in approximately 1615, but underwent major refurbishment in 1899. It is now the headquarters of Chester Civic Trust, who encourage public viewing at specified times.

Below the window are carved panels including the arms of the Sodor and Man (inset).

Both the east and west chambers contain examples of ornate plaster ceilings and period fireplaces.

Night view of Bishop
Lloyd's Palace.

Bishop Lloyd's Palace east chamber with
17th-century ornate plaster and fireplace.

Ornate plaster ceiling and large fireplace located
in the west chamber of Bishop Lloyd's Palace.

Dating from the late 16th century, Watergate Street is reputed to have the oldest British locksmith that is still in business.

Parts of Ye Olde Custom House Inn date from 1637. Formally known as The Star Inn, the name was changed in the 18th century to reflect its position opposite the custom house for the Port of Chester.

The Old Custom House Building at 70 Watergate Street.

The Guildhall is located in the former Holy Trinity Church. Chester's historic Guilds have over 800 years of history and economic influence. Non-guild craftsman or traders were not permitted to work or sell their goods in Chester without paying a levy or attending the summer and autumn fairs. Guild members have revived the ancient tradition of performing the Chester Mystery Plays, which were previously banned in the 1570s – plays are performed every five years. The Guildhall houses a small but interesting museum, which offers free entry to the general public on request.

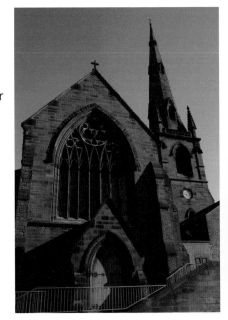

The Guildhall Museum.

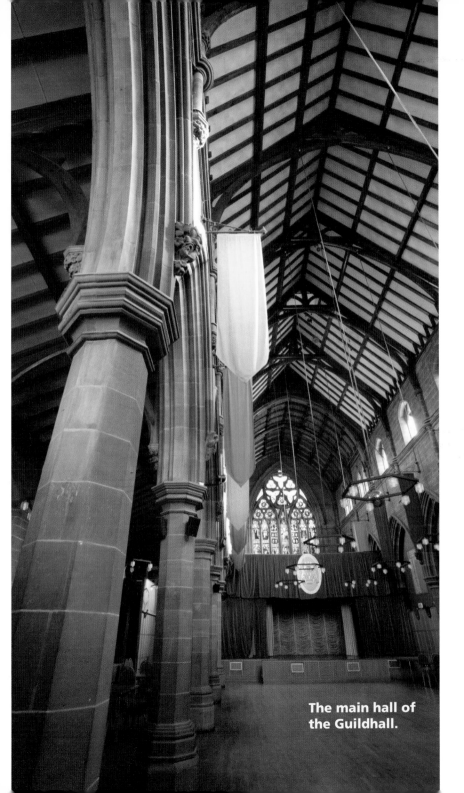

The main hall of the Guildhall.

NORTHGATE STREET AND ST WERBURGH STREET

Northgate Street leads from the centre of the city to the Northgate and Fountains roundabout. In addition to the many retail outlets, cafés, restaurants and pubs, the street offers access to the Forum Shopping Centre, Town Hall and also to the cathedral. Frequent continental and local markets are held in the Market Square.

Timbered black and white Tudor-style building adjoining Eastgate and Northgate Rows.

Originally opened in 1808 as a subscription library, news and coffee room, the Commercial Newsroom was designed in a Greek Revival style by Thomas Harrison, the same architect responsible for the redesign of the Chester Castle complex.

Shoppers on Northgate Street at Shoemakers Row.

A continuation of the north side of Eastgate Row, Northgate Street contains the shortest surviving stretch of Rows in all four galleried row streets. The Northgate Row on the opposite side of the street were demolished, partially to make way for the Commercial Newsroom.

Like other sections of the Chester Rows, Shoemakers' Row was named after the predominant product being produced and traded by its craftsmen.

Black and white building exterior above Northgate Row and retail shops at Shoemakers' Row.

vening view of
hoemaker's Row.

In addition to the Town Hall, the Market Square contains the Forum Shopping Centre and City Council Offices entrance, which are currently subject to a significant redevelopment review.

Although both the Town Hall and Chester Cathedral are located within this area, references to both these locations can be found in their own respective chapters.

Artist Stephen Broadbent created the sculpture *A Celebration of Chester* seen below. Its three figures represent thanksgiving, protection and industry, with protection facing the Town Hall. Thanksgiving is placed centrally between the other two figures and facing towards the cathedral – this is said to represent the 'spiritual life of the individual and the group'. The industry figure reaches downwards to the ground, representing the 'work and effort of every citizen'.

Forum Shopping Centre Market Square entrance, with the Town Hall in the background.

The Tourist Information Centre, which is located at the south end of the Town Hall building.

St Werburgh Street, named after the seventh-century Mercian princess who became a nun and later an Abbess, originally ran from Eastgate Street straight to Chester Cathedral. Today the street leads from the Town Hall Square to Eastgate Street and contains a variety of shops and restaurants. Godstall Lane, a narrow lane leading from St Werburgh back to Eastgate Rows, also contains a selection of cafés, restaurants and shops, where it is possible to dine alfresco with the cathedral as a backdrop.

St Werburgh Street shoe shop sign with Chester Cathedral in the background.

Roman column bases near the library commemorate a European award to Chester for the 'preservation of historic monuments'.

Opposite: Designed by the Odeon's company architect Harry Weedon, the Art Deco-style Odeon Cinema first opened in 1936. The building's future use is uncertain.

The brick and terracotta façade of the former Westminster Coach and Motor Car Works, now the home of Chester Library.

Built in the late 16th or early 17th century and billed as a traditional coaching inn, the Pied Bull Hotel is believed to be Chester's oldest surviving public house that has continuously served beer. There are also rumours that it is haunted.

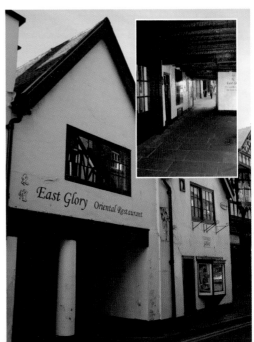

The Blue Bell building dates from the late 15th century. The first recorded licence for the Blue Bell Inn and tavern dates from 1494. This small group of buildings with its arcaded walkway is also known as Lorimer's Row.

Adjacent to the City Wall and Northgate Street, Rufus Court was developed in the early 1950s from a previously derelict and unused part of the city into a small, intimate collection of residential accommodation, cafés, restaurants, shops and offices.

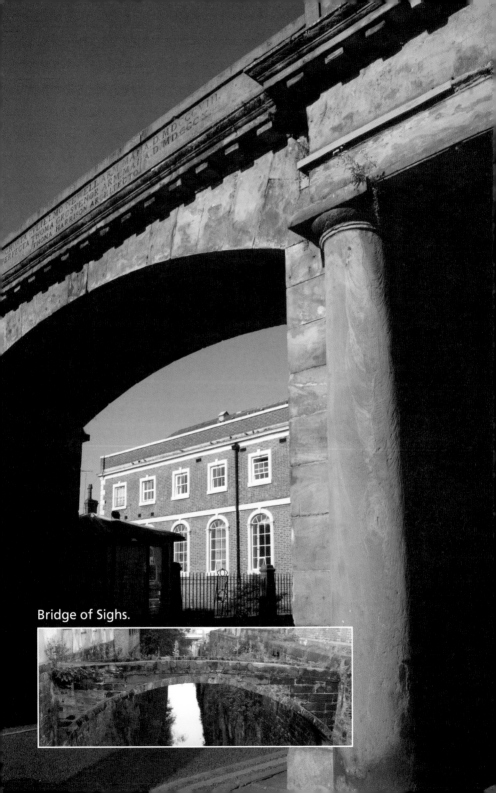

Bridge of Sighs.

Opposite: Rebuilt in 1810, the Northgate's predecessor housed the City Gaol, where a stone footbridge known as the Bridge of Sighs connected the gaol to the chapel of St John in the Blue Coat School. Condemned prisoners are said to have been taken across the bridge to the chapel to receive their last rites. The bridge stretches high above the Chester Canal.

Blue Coat School bell.

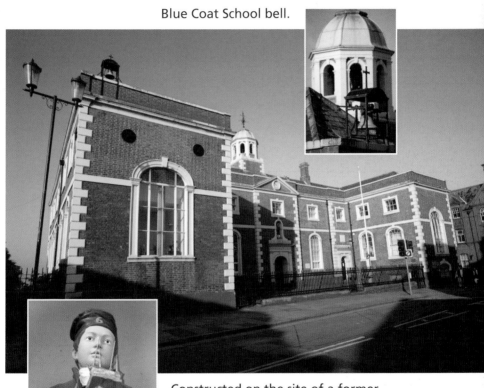

Constructed on the site of a former mediaeval hospital, the Blue Coat School was Chester's oldest purpose-built school. Founded by Bishop Stratford as a charity school for poor boys in 1700, the school is still being utilised as an educational facility for Chester University.

Blue Coat boy statue.

BRIDGE STREET

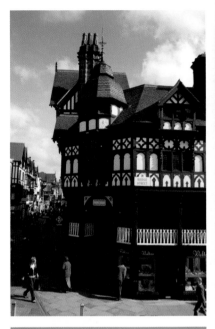

Leading from the High Cross to the Bridgegate at the Old Dee Bridge, via Lower Bridge Street, Bridge Street resumes the retail theme synonymous with the other three streets. The galleried walkways of the Rows extend the whole length on both sides of the street, each connecting with their neighbouring galleried rows on south Eastgate and south Watergate. Almost the entire length of Bridge Street has restricted traffic access, allowing shoppers and workers relatively unrestricted freedom of movement across nearly the whole length and breadth of the street.

Top: The black and white timbered Tudor-style reconstructed buildings at The Cross are believed to be the most photographed scene, after the Eastgate Clock, in Chester.

Galleried Rows on the west side of Bridge Street.

Eastgate and Bridge Street junction at High Cross.

Shop signs on Bridge Street.

Shop front of the 13th-century crypt at 12 Bridge Street.

The 13th-century crypt at 12 Bridge Street is thought to be one of the oldest in the city. It is now being utilised as a high-class handbag, footwear and accessories boutique.

Built in the late 17th century, the Dutch Houses on the west side of Bridge Street are so-named because of the possible Dutch design influence.

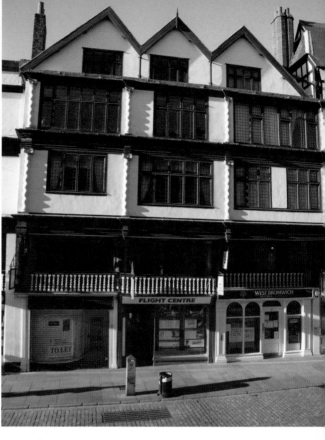

Bridge Street Rows with the Dutch Houses above.

Grosvenor Shopping Centre, Bridge Street entrance.

Built for the second Duke of Westminster in 1910, the Grosvenor Shopping Centre's original tiled façade met with fierce public disapproval, eventually leading to the tiles being replaced with the current timber-framed frontage. However, the tiles of the Edwardian arcade of St Michael's Row were retained.

Grosvenor Shopping Centre's Bridge Street entrance leads to St Michael's Row. This elegant arcade contains a range of quality retailers including gents and ladies outfitters, fashion boutiques, jewellery shops and an art gallery.

Below: St Michael's Row tiled façade.

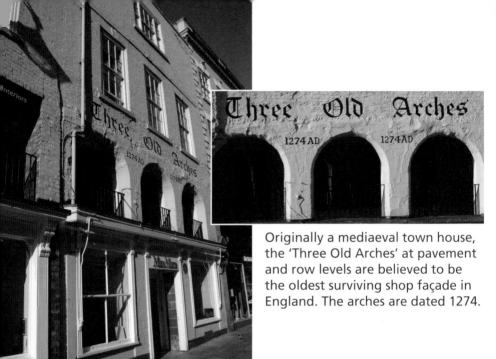

Originally a mediaeval town house, the 'Three Old Arches' at pavement and row levels are believed to be the oldest surviving shop façade in England. The arches are dated 1274.

Built in 1822 for an art dealer, the façade of this building contains a carving of King Charles I. When the carpenters came to install the carving they found that it was too tall for its recess and had to shorten the legs to make it fit.

St Michael's Church opened as Britain's first Heritage Centre in 1975. The church was one of nine mediaeval parish churches of Chester and stands on the site of the Roman fortress southern gateway.

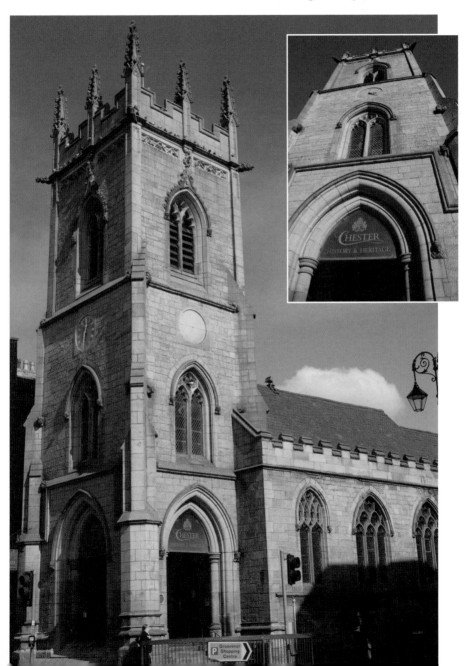

Lower Bridge Street

Lower Bridge Street Rows have all but disappeared. The retail outlets tend to be more specialist and unique and are mixed with an excellent combination of cafés, bars and restaurants distributed throughout the length of the street.

After falling into a derelict state the Falcon Inn was restored and formally reopened by  the Duke of Westminster in 1992. During its long history the structure has been utilised for many purposes and is recorded as the first building to have its Rows enclosed to create more private living space for its residents.

Tudor House, a timber-framed town house, was constructed in the early 1600s for a wealthy merchant.
A plaque on the wall dating the build as 1503 is thought to be incorrect.

Park House, with its Doric entrance porch.

A Georgian town house dating from 1717, Park House has undergone many changes of use from its initial purpose as a private residence including a hotel, ladies' academy, antiques emporium, wine bar and offices. The Duke of Wellington reputedly stayed in the building when it was being used as the Albion Hotel in 1820.

There are several public houses on Lower Bridge Street, some of which have a varied history of use.

Ye Olde Kings Head is much older than its first licence to sell alcohol, which was granted 1717.

The Cross Keys is a traditional pub.

A mediaeval timber-framed building 'Dollectable', ia being used as an an antique doll shop. This is an example of the specialist retail shops on Lower Bridge Street.

Deconsecrated, St Olave's Church was supposedly named after King Olave of Norway, who died in 1030.

Built in the late 18th century, this row of houses on Lower Bridge Street's Bridge Place is an example of Georgian architecture.

Now a public house and restaurant, the Bear and Billet on Lower Bridge Street is named after the Earl of Shrewsbury's heraldic device of a shackled bear. Believed to be designed in a similar style to a Dutch merchant's house, the building dates from 1664.

St Mary's Hill is a small lane near the bottom of Lower Bridge Street. It is reputedly the steepest cobbled street in England. At the top of the street is St Mary's on the Hill Church, which is no longer used as a parish church.

St Mary's Hill and a silhouette view of St Mary's Church.

HIGH CROSS

Chester High Cross dates from approximately 1377. The Parliamentarians deliberately demolished the original cross after the Civil War. Partially restored and retained in the Roman Gardens, the High Cross was finally returned to its city centre location in 1975, although parts of the original structure have never been recovered.

The High Cross.

CHESTER TOWN CRIER

The ancient tradition of reading Noon Proclamations from Chester High Cross dates from the 16th century. Although the ritual ceased in the late 19th century, the position of Chester Town Crier was re-established in 1978. Today this tradition is performed by Chester Town Crier David Mitchell, who reads Noon Proclamations at Chester's High Cross on a Tuesday to Saturday from May to August.

The Town Crier demonstrating the use of the stocks to a passing volunteer.

Chester Town Crier at the High Cross.

CHESTER CITY WALLS

Often referred to as 'The Walled City' and at just over 3km (approximately two miles) in length, Chester has the most complete circuit of walls in Britain. A walk along the City Wall will reveal a fascinating history that spans from its Roman fortress of Deva origins through the Saxon and mediaeval periods until the more recent cosmetic alterations to transform the wall from its original protective role to a fashionable and popular promenade with Georgian and Victorian origins. The ramparts still bear the scars of cannon bombardment and defence breaches. There is lots to see on and from the wall, with spectacular elevated views of the city streets, Roman Amphitheatre, Old Dee Bridge, River Dee, Chester Canal, Roman Gardens and even magnificent views across to Wales. In recognition of their archaeological importance, Chester City Walls have been designated as a Scheduled Ancient Monument. Chester City Council, in partnership with Chester

Civic Trust, has established a highly recommended and informative 'City Wall Heritage Trail'.

The following images illustrate a few of the vistas and points of interest.

It is possible to join and leave the wall walk in many locations. However, the images have been presented in a clockwise route starting and finishing at the Eastgate Clock.

Standing on top of the Eastgate and below the Eastgate Clock, is an ideal location for admiring the different styles of architecture along Eastgate Street.

Eastgate Clock with the City Wall route and Eastgate Street in the background.

Built in the late 1930s as part of a city traffic enhancement scheme, the Newgate offers a good view of the Chester Visitor Centre and the excavation works at the Roman Amphitheatre.

View of the Roman Amphitheatre from Newgate.

Adjacent to the Newgate is the 17th-century Wolfgate and the remains of a Roman Angle Tower.

View of the Roman Gardens from the Newgate.

Built in 1949, the Roman Gardens were created to display an array of Roman columns and bases that had been discovered throughout the city. There are often Roman tours being conducted in the garden, which is also a popular place of respite for city workers and visitors alike.

Evening view of the Nine Houses and the wall walkway.

Constructed as almshouses, the 'Nine Houses' on Chester's Park Street are clearly visible from the wall. Of the original nine mid-17th-century dwellings, only six are now remaining.

The Watch Tower was subject to fierce attack and sniper fire during the Civil War. Indeed, the base of the tower still bears the scars of cannonball bombardment.

Opposite: Constructed as part of a promenade project in 1785, the Wishing Steps join two different levels of the wall. Folklore states that if you run up and down the Wishing Steps without taking a breath, then your wish will come true. This is apparently a particularly popular myth among ladies who are seeking wedlock.

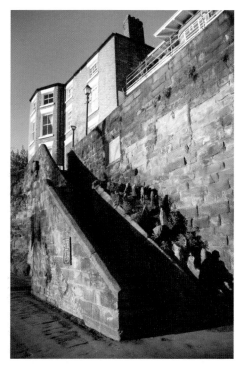

It is believed that the original Recorder Steps were added to the wall in the early 1700s, allowing access between the wall and Groves. Talented artists can be found displaying their creative works at the bottom of the steps.

The Round Tower.

Utilised as a mediaeval watch tower, the elevated position of the Round Tower offers superb views over the Norman weir, River Dee and the Old Dee Bridge towards Edgar's Field.

Opposite: The Round Tower with the River Dee in the background.

Built in 1782, the Bridgegate was designed by Joseph Turner, who was also responsible for the Watergate. Being the only mediaeval route from the city into North Wales ensured that the Bridgegate's predecessors, also known as the Welshgate and South Gate, were heavily fortified and defended. Previous gates also contained a water tank that supplied the city with fresh water.

View over the Norman weir with the wall and Bridgegate in the background.

Bas-relief of a balance carved in the stonework of the Bridgegate with the gate balustrades above.

County Hall was built on the site of the former gaol. Although construction of the building began in the 1930s it was not totally completed until 1957. The wall route passes the front of the County Hall, but the section of wall at Castle Drive was altered in 1901 when the wall walk was re-routed.

Chester Castle walls and motte. The castle was originally built by the Normans in approximately 1070.

Chester Racecourse, also known as the Roodee, with the City Wall on the right.

Top of the Watergate and City Wall route with Watergate Street in the background.

The Watergate (1788) built by the Bridgegate designer Joseph Turner replaced a mediaeval West Gate. Prior to the silting up of the River Dee the water course ran adjacent to the City Walls at this point.

Sedan House, so named because of its two-door porch, which allowed the bearers of a sedan chair to enter the building through one door and stop outside the facing door, thus allowing a passenger to alight inside the building.

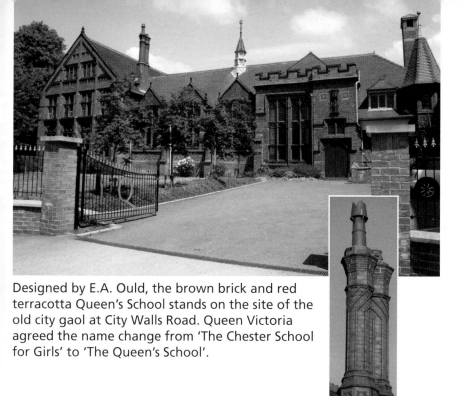

Designed by E.A. Ould, the brown brick and red terracotta Queen's School stands on the site of the old city gaol at City Walls Road. Queen Victoria agreed the name change from 'The Chester School for Girls' to 'The Queen's School'.

Infirmary sign and arched window with gold-painted 'ERECTED 1761' inscription.

The site of the former Chester Royal Infirmary on City Walls Road has now been converted to luxury residential apartments. Royal was added to the infirmary name after King George V opened a new wing of the hospital in 1914.

Utilised as a watch tower, Bonewaldesthorne's Tower was originally located at the banks of the River Dee. Silting of the river made it necessary to build another watch tower in 1322. The Water Tower is placed on a spur wall from Bonewaldesthome's Tower to the then location of the river. As the river further silted and receded, the Water Tower was also left stranded.

A better view of the Water Tower can be achieved from the Water Tower Gardens, which can be reached via nearby steps.

Bonewaldesthorne's Tower on the City Wall.

Chester Canal basin viewed from the City Wall. Part of the Shropshire Union Canal, Chester Canal runs parallel with this section of the City Wall.

Pemberton's Parlour is the site of a mediaeval watch tower. The tower is named after the owner of a rope works, who would survey his workers as they laboured below. However, the tower has previously been named Dille's Tower and Goblin Tower. An inscription on the stone states that it was rebuilt in 1894.

Morgan's Mount is a watch tower that is believed to have been named after Captain Morgan, a Royalist gun battery commander who defended the city from this position during the Civil War, 1642–46.

Inscription on top of the Northgate. Built by Thomas Harrison in 1810, the arched Northgate replaced a former mediaeval gate.

Local legend states that King Charles stood on this tower and witnessed his army being defeated, or pursued, by Parliamentary troops during the battle of Rowton Moor in 1645. Also known as Phoenix Tower, there is a carved stone phoenix which was the emblem of Chester's Guild of Painters.

KING CHARLES
STOOD ON THIS TOWER
SEPT. 24. 1645. AND SAW
HIS ARMY DEFEATED
ON ROWTON MOOR

Steps and inscription (inset)
on King Charles Tower.

The Chester Cathedral Addleshaw Bell Tower, viewed from the wall.

Returning to the Eastgate Clock completes the City Wall circuit. Some of the views from the wall including the Roman Garden, River Dee, Chester Castle, Water Tower Garden, Chester Canal, Chester Cathedral and some street views are illustrated further within their own chapters.

CHESTER CASTLE

Chester Castle consists of an outer and inner bailey. After the complex underwent major development during the 18th and 19th centuries, little now remains of the mediaeval castle's original outer bailey. Thomas Harrison, the architect responsible for the redesign, replaced the dilapidated mediaeval gaol and Shire Hall, previously known as the Great Hall, with a much-admired group of Greek revival buildings fronted by an impressive propylaeum-style gateway. The building project began in a piecemeal fashion in 1788 but was not fully completed until 1822.

Queen Victoria's statue in front of Chester Crown Court.

Queen Victoria's statue and Chester Crown Court viewed from the gateway.

Castle Gateway.

Castle entrance to County Hall with St Mary's on the Hill church tower in the background.

Chester Castle's Harrison Block is home to the Cheshire Military Museum. The museum contains exhibits relating to the Cheshire Regiment, Cheshire Yeomanry, 5th Royal Inniskilling Dragoon Guards, 3rd Carabiniers, Eaton Hall Officer Cadet School and other smaller military Cheshire units.

Some semblance of mediaeval history is still evident within Chester Castle's inner bailey, c.1150. The Agricola Tower, also known as Julius Caesar's Tower and Julius Agricola's Tower, stands at the entrance to the inner bailey.

Napier House, armoury, designed by Captain Kitson, is situated adjacent to the inner bailey wall.

CHESTER CATHEDRAL

From the Saxon Minster to the Benedictine Abbey of Saint Werburgh, worship has taken place on the site of Chester Cathedral for over 1,000 years. Chester Cathedral was transformed from the former Benedictine Abbey of St Werburgh and was founded as a cathedral by Henry VIII in 1541. The building and site have undergone many transformations but the cathedral is said to 'contain materials from every Christian century since the tenth'. Major restoration during the late 1800s and again in the 1900s has changed the appearance of the cathedral and also caused some architectural controversy. Chester Cathedral is officially known as the Cathedral of Christ and the Blessed Virgin Mary.

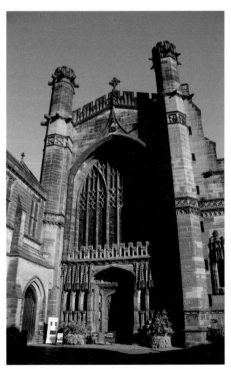 

Located at the junction of Northgate Street and St Werburgh Street, the cathedral, a magnificent tourist attraction and important place of worship, has been open to tourists for almost 100 years.

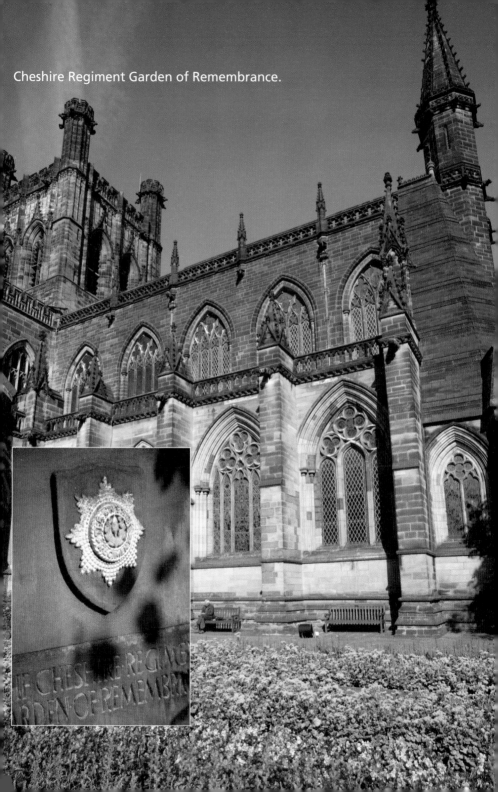
Cheshire Regiment Garden of Remembrance.

Designed by George Pace, the Chester Cathedral Addleshaw Bell Tower was named after a cathedral Dean. The tower was built in 1975 after it was discovered that the cathedral's own tower was no longer able to support the bells. Located in the cathedral gardens, it is said to be the first bell tower to be built separately from an English cathedral since the 1600s.

Internal viewing of the cathedral will reveal many original Norman and late mediaeval features. There is a magnificent selection of new and old stained-glass windows. Look closely and you will also see the Chester Imp carved into the stone near one of the nave windows – the figure is said to frighten the Devil away.

Opposite: Stained-glass of the west window, Chester Cathedral.

The Chester Imp.

Nave roof bosses.

Chester
Cathedral nave
looking east.

The organ and Quire entrance in Chester Cathedral Tower.

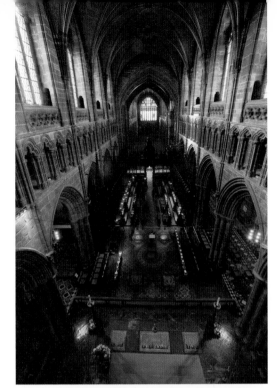

There is a fascinating collection of mediaeval oak carvings in the Quire. One example of a wooden elephant was obviously carved by a craftsman who had never seen the real animal, believing that an elephant had the same legs and hooves as a horse.

The High Altar.

Overleaf: Roof bosses above the Quire.

SERAPHIM

Carving of Christ on the Cross, above the Quire entrance.

Opposite: Shrine of Saint Werburgh located in the Lady Chapel.

The 14th-century Abbey Gateway leads from Northgate Street to Abbey Square. This was the former site of the Abbey brewhouse and bakery, which was converted by the cathedral in the 18th century to a square of smart residential properties. The cobbled street is lined with parallel tracks of York stone paving, known as wheelers, designed to assist the transit of horse and carriage.

Bishop of Chester's residence at 1 Abbey Square.

ST JOHN'S CHURCH

One of the oldest religious sites in Chester, this former Saxon Minster, now the Church of St John the Baptist, is believed to date from the seventh century, making it one of Chester's oldest surviving structures. St John's became Chester's first cathedral in 1075, but only remained so until 1102. Evidence suggests that the original structure of the church was built with materials taken from the nearby Roman amphitheatre. Restoration work in the 19th century gave this Norman church a Victorian appearance. Ruins at both sides of St John's are from previous tower collapses dating from the 14th, 15th and 19th centuries.

Rear exterior view of St John's.

St John's ruins with the clock tower in the background.

North West Tower ruins at St John's.

Until its collapse, the great North West Tower and belfry of St John's was nearly three times higher than any other city landmark. The tower was said to dominate the Chester skyline. This tower was also used as a sniper position and cannon emplacement for the attacking Parliamentarian army during the Civil War. The firing of cannons may have contributed to the weakening of the structure and its eventual collapse on Good Friday, 15 April 1881.

Some would argue that the real splendour of this magnificent structure is best appreciated from inside the church, where much of its Norman heritage is still evident.

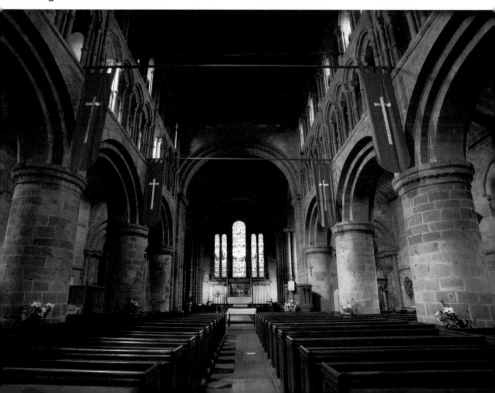

A 14th-century painting of St John the Baptist is still visible on one of the pillars.

Opposite: Among St John's more modern acquisitions is one of the organs used for Queen Victoria's Coronation at Westminster Abbey in 1838. The organ was purchased after the great event and transported to its current location.

CHESTER TOWN HALL

Designed by the Belfast architect W.H. Lynn, Chester Town Hall was opened in the late 19th century by the Prince of Wales with the Prime Minister of that time, W.E. Gladstone, in attendance.

Opposite: The impressive façade of this Victorian Gothic-style building has an equally striking interior. The staircase has Victorian stained-glass windows depicting a series of Chester Earls from the previous 1,000 years.

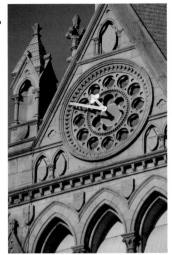

The Town Hall clock.

The staircase from ground

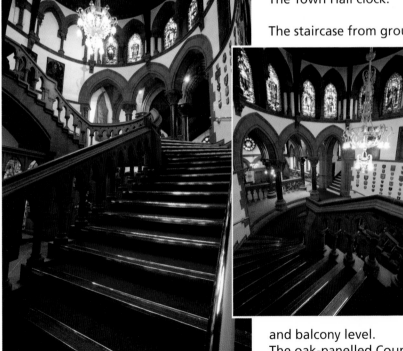

and balcony level.
The oak-panelled Council

134

Chester Town Hall with the
Celebration of Chester
thanksgiving, protection
and industry sculpture at
Market Square.

Chambers is an impressive room. The former armorial bearings of Chester and the Earl of Chester's coat of arms (bottom left and middle) are displayed above the fireplaces (opposite).

The gallery clock (bottom right) in the Council Chambers is inscribed with the date that the chamber was destroyed by fire in 1897 and restored the following year.

The Lord Mayoral Suite contains the Mayor's Parlour (above), and the Lady Mayoress's Parlour (above right), which are used for the reception of civic visitors.

The Assembly Room is the largest room in the Town Hall. Its walls are decorated with grand paintings of former Dukes of Westminster and photographs of past Lord Mayors.

LORD MAYOR AND SHERIFF OF CHESTER

Chairman of the City Council, the Lord Mayor of Chester's role is primarily ceremonial. This differs tremendously from the Mayor's responsibility when the position was first established in the 13th century. Then the Mayor passed local laws, enforced law and order and governed the social and economic life of the Chester inhabitants. In recognition of its 'historical and economical importance' HM the Queen granted Lord Mayoralty status to Chester in 1992, which included a title change for the Lord Mayor to The Right Worshipful, the Lord Mayor of the City of Chester.

Councillor James Latham, The Right Worshipful Lord Mayor of The City of Chester.

Dating back to the 12th century, Chester is believed to be the first English town to have had a Sheriff. Indeed, until the position was disbanded in 1835, Chester had two Sheriffs, each with their own legal responsibilities for controlling the city gaol, collecting tolls and fines, executing writs and assisting the courts. In 1974 a change in Borough status allowed the Council to resurrect the appointment of a Sheriff.

The Sheriff of Chester, Councillor Andrew Storrar.

Lord Mayor's
ceremonial
procession a
the Town Ha

Attending official ceremonies occasionally requires the Lord Mayor to be escorted by civic staff and be adorned with regalia including a magnificent sword, scabbard and mace dating from the 15th and 17th centuries.

Ceremonial sword bearing the inscription 'Charles Earl of Derby', with the date of presentation 1668.

Ceremonial mace.

CHESTER RACECOURSE

Dating from the 16th century, Chester Racecourse on the Roodee is reputed to be the oldest racecourse in England. Its circular layout ensures that race-goers have the unique visual advantage of being able to see

the whole course without the aid of binoculars – the oval-shaped course also earned it the nickname of 'Soup-Plate'. Situated on the former Roman port, the course aptly illustrates how the river has changed course over the centuries.

Aerial view of Chester Racecourse.

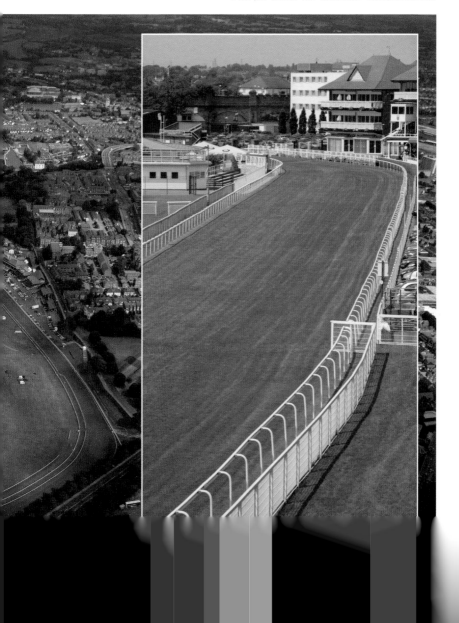

CHESTER CANAL

Continual silting of the River Dee, combined with the development of the Port of Liverpool and other major canal construction projects, began to undermine Chester's position as a major sea port. This threat to its sea trade partially provided the impetus to build a canal link from Chester to Nantwich.

Work began on the canal in 1772 but the whole project was fraught with financial, engineering and planning problems. Although not the original planned route, a 16-mile Chester to Nantwich canal was finally completed in 1779. However, the project was considered an economic failure. It was not until the expansion of a link between Chester and

Chester canal basin and lock, connecting the canal to the River Dee.

Ellesmere Port, which now forms part of the Shropshire Union Canal, in the late 18th century, that the canal established itself as successful commercial venture. The Ellesmere Port link became an extremely popular and profitable passenger and cargo route. The arrival of a railway link to Chester in 1840 created competition for the canal and eventually led to its commercial demise. However, there have been new initiatives to regenerate the canal routes for leisure and sporting activities, both on the canal's water and its towpath.

Designed by Thomas Telford, Telford's Warehouse was constructed to allow the loading and unloading of canal boats directly into the warehouse from an arched waterway thoroughfare.

Canal boat heading towards the city centre.

Decades of tow rope use have left telltale
indentations on this canal path iron bar.

Built in 1834, the Steam Mill was a former seed warehouse that is now being utilised as an office block.

Canal-side residential and office development has combined the old and new. Previously derelict buildings are being redeveloped and given a new lease of life.

Leadworks Tower was built for the manufacture of lead shot. Droplets of molten lead would become sphere-shaped as they fell from the top of the tower into a barrel of cooling water.

PARKS AND GARDENS

Grosvenor Park

Grosvenor Park is a 19th-century Victorian-designed 20-acre public recreational area. Opened in 1867, the park was originally gifted to the city by Richard Grosvenor, the 2nd Marquis of Westminster.

Grosvenor Park Lodge is located at the Grosvenor Park Road and Union Street junction entrance. Originally known as the Park Keeper's Lodge, this black and white half-timbered building was designed by John Douglas, who also designed the Eastgate Clock. The building is decorated with wood carvings of William the Conqueror and the Norman Earls of Chester (see page 152).

Grosvenor Park tree-lined avenue, with a statue of Richard Grosvenor, the 2nd Marquis of Westminster, in the background.

The Park Keeper's lodge.

A close-up view of the wood carvings on the Park Keeper's lodge.

Billy Hobby's Well on the edge of Grosvenor Park has an ancient tradition whereby, maidens would stand with their right leg immersed in the water of the well and wish for a husband.

Grosvenor Park Miniature Railway is a popular attraction for young and old alike. The operators run a selection of steam and diesel engines at predetermined days and times.

St Michael's Arch with St Mary's Arch in the background. The park contains ancient arches that have been relocated from their original sites, including the former west door of St Michael's Church.

Water Tower Gardens

The Water Tower was constructed on the edge of the Dee. As the river changed course and receded the tower was left high and dry. Built on the reclaimed land during the Victorian period, Water Tower Gardens is a designated conservation area. The park contains facilities for the local community to use including a bowling green, tennis courts and pavilion. There is also a Roman-influenced dolphin mosaic at the centre of a coloured maze.

Water Tower Garden maze with the Water Tower in the background.

Opposite: Steps from the City Wall to the Water Tower Gardens, with the Water Tower Maze and bowling green in the background.

View of Bonewaldesthorne's Tower
from Water Tower Garden.

Edgar's Field

Named after King Edgar, who ascended to the throne in 959, Edgar's Field was donated to Chester as a public park by the 1st Duke of Westminster in 1892. The park contains the Roman shrine to the goddess Minerva. Adjacent to the River Dee, this 2¼ acre recreational area affords excellent views over the river towards the Old Dee Bridge and city.

Minerva's Shrine.

Evening view of the Roman Gardens with the City Wall in the background.

Roman Gardens

Constructed in 1949 adjacent to the City Wall, the Roman Gardens is a secluded location that proves to be a popular tourist attraction and lunchtime haunt for city workers. In addition to the various Roman columns and bases there is also a reconstructed hypocaust (underfloor heating system). The artefacts and information plates in the top part of the garden are intended to provide an enhanced educational experience, especially for the many school groups that visit the area. Many of the plants, shrubs and trees contained within the formal garden have a Roman theme or association.

The reconstructed hypocaust.

Roman tour in the Roman Gardens.

Grosvenor Museum

Named after the 1st Duke of Westminster, Lupus Grosvenor, the Grosvenor Museum was built in 1885–86. Domineered by an impressive life-size Roman Centurion, adopting aggressive stance, the entrance hallway leads to a variety of ground and upper level display exhibitions and galleries.

The museum is especially renowned for 'the largest collection of Roman tombstones from a single site', exhibited in the Webster Roman Stones Gallery. Before being recovered and displayed at the museum, virtually all of the tombstones had been utilised to repair the City Wall.

The life-size Roman Centurion in the museum's entrance hallway.

Above left: Originally established in 1701, an Act of Parliament closed Chester's Assay Office in 1962. The city's long association with silver is beautifully displayed within the Museum's Ridgway Silver Gallery.

Above right: The 'Art in Chester' Gallery contains a collection of fine art drawings, sculptures, watercolours, paintings and prints.

'A House Through Time' exhibition within the Period House area of the museum aptly illustrates life in a gentry townhouse during different eras. Pictured below are the Victorian Parlour and Period House Kitchen, *c.*1900.

CHESTER ZOO

There are over 7,000 animals and 500 species at Chester Zoo's 110-acre zoological gardens. Located three miles from the city centre, Britain's largest garden zoo is an award-winning and extremely popular visitor attraction that is renowned for its conservation outreach programmes.

Elephants.

Feeding time at the Lion's Den.

Giraffe.

Zoofari
overhead
railway.

Penguins.   Sea Lion.

PLACES OF INTEREST

The city contains an abundance of structures and areas of interest that merit a detour from the principal thoroughfares. The following pages contain a few of the many examples that are worthy of mention or exploration.

Chester City Football Club

Nicknamed the Blues or City, Chester City Football Club was founded as Chester FC in 1885. The club play their home games at the Deva Stadium on the Sealand Estate. Situated on the border of England and Wales, part of this English FC site is actually located in Wales.

Chester FC versus Milton Keynes Dons.

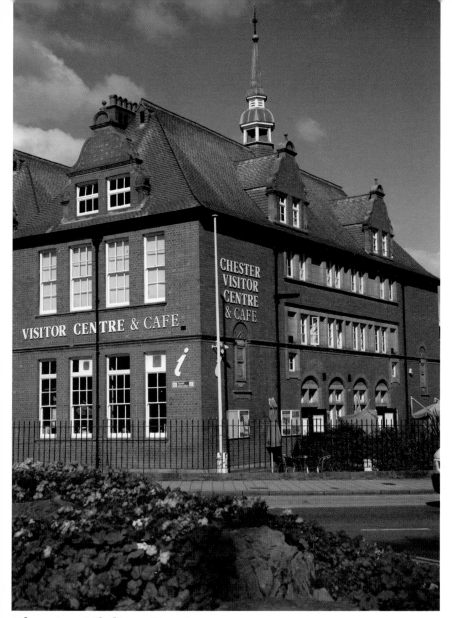

Chester Visitor Centre

Located at Vicars Lane opposite the amphitheatre, Chester Visitor Centre was formerly Grosvenor St John's School and is now a Visitor Welcome facility.

City Baths

Chester established its first public baths in 1849 which were replaced by floating baths on the River Dee in 1883. The Union Street City Baths were opened in 1901. This stone, brick and half-timbered building was designed by Harold Burgess, but completed by John Douglas.

Chester Indoor Market

Chester indoor market is currently located near the Town Hall in Princess Street, but is scheduled for relocation. The market traders offer an array of goods for sale from fresh fruit and vegetables to bales of cloth.

Railway Station

Chester General Station was constructed in the mid-19th century by the celebrated civil engineer contractor Thomas Brassey. The 354-metre fronted building was designed in an Italianate style by Francis Thompson.

Marlbororough Arms

The reputedly haunted Marlbororough Arms in St John Street credits the unique spelling of its name to a signwriter who either had too much to drink, or was paid by the letter.

CHESTER TOURS

Roman Centurions.

There are a variety of accredited guides and commercial organisations that provide well-informed tours of the city.

Companies like Roman Tours Ltd offer guided educational tours to both school groups and adults. The Deva Victrix leg of Roman Tours also conducts a series of open-air Roman re-enactments throughout the year.

Roman funeral re-enactment (Festival of Pomonia, Funeral Parade for a Gladiator).

Chester Heritage Tours provide visitors with an open-top bus tour in a replica vintage B-Type motorbus.

Young Roman recruit wearing Roman attire.

CHESTER AT CHRISTMAS

An already attractive city setting for workers, shoppers and visitors, Chester's streets take on a truly magical appearance over the festive season. The streets are adorned with Christmas decorations and lights while the Market Square becomes home to continental and local market traders, selling a wide selection of merchandise and exotic produce.

Christmas parade at Shoemakers Row on Northgate Street.

Carol singing at Market Square with the Town Hall in the background.

Christmas lights at the Eastgate Clock.

Opposite: High Cross with the Eastgate and Bridge Street junction in the background.

BEYOND THE WALLS

Beyond Chester's city walls and boundaries, the county of Cheshire contains many magnificent rural scenes, landscapes, locations and visitor attractions that are worthy of mention. Here are just a few of them.

Cheshire Oaks

Situated on the outskirts of the City of Chester near Ellesmere Port, Cheshire Oaks is the largest designer outlet in the UK. With over 140 shops and stores, plus a large entertainment complex, Cheshire Oaks attracts nearly seven million shoppers each year. This is a popular venue for both visitors and Cheshire residents.

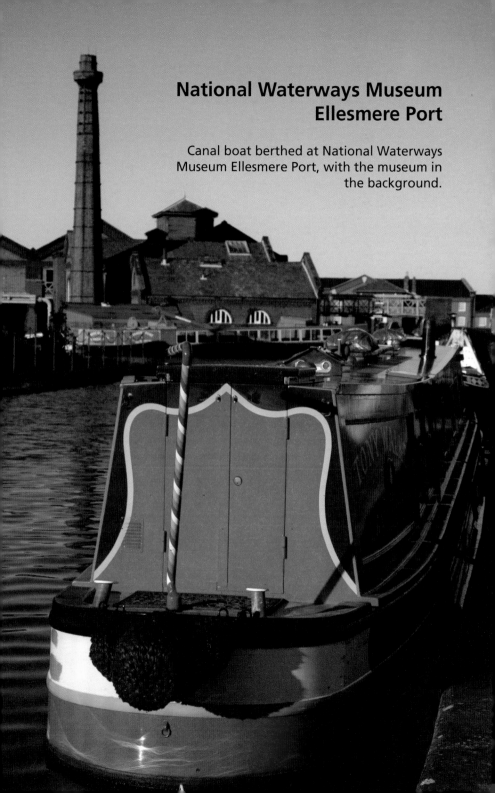

National Waterways Museum Ellesmere Port

Canal boat berthed at National Waterways Museum Ellesmere Port, with the museum in the background.

Located approximately eight miles from Chester, the National Waterways Museum Ellesmere Port, formerly the Boat Museum, is home to the largest collection of floating canal boats in the world. Situated on the banks of the River Mersey, within an 18th-century dock complex, the museum offers a range of traditional on and off water exhibits, plus modern interactive displays. A working blacksmith's forge and canal boat river trips further enhance the visitor experience.

Below: Canal boat exhibition hall.

Malpas Yesteryear Rally

Fourteen miles south of Chester on the A41, Malpas stages an annual yesteryear rally that attracts approximately 20,000 visitors every year. Since its formation in 1972, the late summer weekend gathering brings together vintage transport enthusiasts from all over the UK. The event plays host to impressive collections of classic cars, steam-driven farming and industrial machinery, bygone public transport, fairground amusements and much more.

Cheshire Farm Ice Cream

One of the largest ice cream parlours in the country, Cheshire Farm Ice Cream offers a fantastic range of award-winning farm-produced ice cream. With a superb range of ice cream flavours, visitors to this free admission attraction have the opportunity to view cows being milked from a specially erected 'milking viewing gallery' and visit the animal corner. A birds of prey exhibition, which incurs a small nominal charge, and a free children's adventure playground add further excitement to a truly tasty visit.

An owl from the birds of prey exhibition.

The adventure playground.

CHESHIRE FARM

AL DAIRY

CREAM

Port Sunlight Village

A designated conservation area within the Cheshire boundaries and located approximately 15 miles from the city of Chester, Port Sunlight Village was initially founded in 1888 by the entrepreneur soap manufacturer and philanthropist, Lord Leverhulme. With differing building materials and design styles the project is said to be influenced by the work of over 30 architects, with the whole development being scrupulously supervised by Lord Leverhulme. The village was created to provide a good standard of affordable accommodation for the soap factory workers. However, residents had to abide by a strict code of temperance and compulsory participation in company activities. Believing in betterment for his workers and their families, Lord Leverhulme's model community also provided recreation, educational, cultural, church and medical facilities.

Lady Lever Art Gallery

Founded by Lord William Hesketh Leverhulme in memory of his wife Elizabeth Hulme, the Lady Lever Art Gallery is renowned for its furniture, porcelain and art exhibitions, which include works by Turner and Constable. Opened in 1922 by Queen Victoria's daughter Princess Beatrice, the gallery is said to have been established to enrich the cultural and educational awareness of his employees, and the general public. Visitors also have an opportunity to relax or shop in the galleries gift shop and Lady Lever café.

CHESHIRE LANDSCAPES

Rural seasonal landscape scenes of the Cheshire villages of Coddington and Aldersey.

ACKNOWLEDGEMENTS

We would like to acknowledge the significant contribution and support of the following people who have so very kindly provided assistance during the writing of this book. Without the extensive co-operation of both the personnel and organisations, we would have been unable to create such a detailed portfolio of images that portray the beauty of Chester.

His Grace the Duke of Westminster, Rachael Ashton, Sue Carmichael, Reverend David Chesters, Penta Clark, Christine Cunliffe, Cameron and James Cundill, Lesley Falshaw, Nicholas Fry, Nigel Hine, Paul Harston, Susan Hughes, Dennis Johnson, The Lord Mayor James Latham, David Mitchell, Andy Noller, Rebecca Pinfold, Emma Plazalska, Sally Poulter, David Serjup, Sheriff of Chester Councillor Andrew Storrar, Peter Thompson, Chris Turner, Alison Watson, Helen Williams and Julie Williams.

Cheshire Farm Ice Cream
Cheshire Military Museum
Cheshire Oaks Designer Outlet – managed by McArthurGlen
Chester Cathedral
Chester City Council
Chester Civic Trust
Chester Football Club
Chester Grosvenor and Spa
Chester Guildhall
Chester Heritage Tours
Chester History and Heritage
Chester Indoor Market
Chester Town Hall
Chester Zoo
Cruise
Grosvenor Museum
National Waterways Museum – Ellesmere Port
St John's Church
The Mall, Chester
Town Crier
Roman Tours
Yesteryear Malpas Steam Rally

And a special thanks to our proofreaders, Jacqui and Karl Cundill, Muriel and Ken Green, Elaine Pierce-Jones, Pam Lynch and Alison Watson.